PENN'S CREEK

PENN'S CREEK

Daniel L. Shields

Photography by: Walt Young

Frank Amato

PORTLAND

River Journal

Volume 3, Number 4, 1995

Dan Shields caught his first fish at age four, on cane pole and worm, under the watchful eye of his grandfather, Paul Kramer. Since then, he has fished wherever and whenever possible. His itch for the sport was well scratched when he attended Penn State University, which is in close proximity to the Keystone State's best trout streams. After graduating, Dan lived in Hawaii and Arizona, but always managed to return to his beloved Centre County streams in time for trout season. An opportunity to work at Flyfisher's Paradise, the fly shop servicing Central Pennsylvania, turned into a partnership in the business. Dan and his wife, Lynn, live in Centre County, a stone's throw away from one of the region's many fine limestone trout streams.

◆

Acknowledgments

Lynn Shields, Mark Ralston, George Harvey, Joe Humphreys, David Johnson, Steve Sywensky, Ernie Erdeky, Fred Johnson, Greg Hoover, Pennsylvania Fish and Boat Commission Fisheries Bureau staff, Bill Glaus, Paul Hutchison, Penn's Cave, Woodward Cave, Maria Davidson, Walt Young, Helen Fahy, Bill van den Berg, Bob Laubach, Centre County Library staff, Frank Zettle, George "The Gypsy" Lukas, Bob Hohn, Bernie Robb, Mark Antolosky, Dave Carson, and all of the generous landowners along Penn's Creek who welcome anglers.

Dedicated to Paul Kramer, who took a small boy fishing.

◆

Series Editor: Frank Amato

Subscriptions:
Softbound: $35.00 for one year (four issues)
$65.00 for two years
Hardbound Limited Editions: $95.00 one year, $170.00 for two years
Frank Amato Publications, Inc. • P.O. Box 82112 • Portland, Oregon 97282 • (503) 653-8108

Design: Alan Reid
Photography: Walt Young
Map: Alan Reid
Printed in Hong Kong
Softbound ISBN:1-57188-008-9, Hardbound ISBN:1-57188-009-7
(Hardbound Edition Limited to 500 Copies)

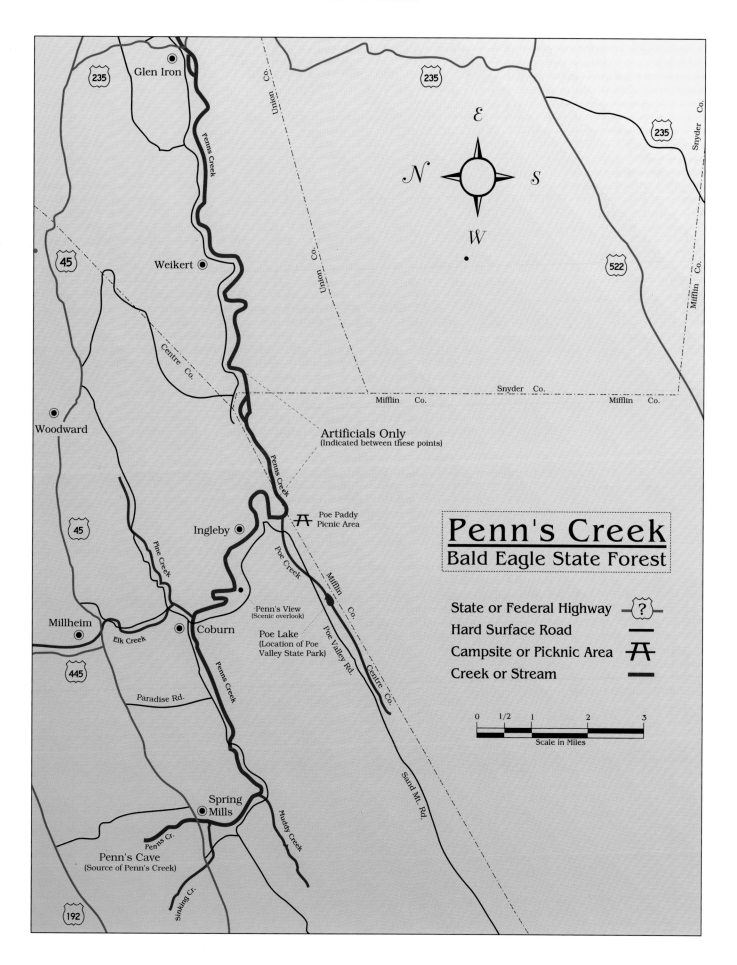

Penn's Creek
Bald Eagle State Forest

State or Federal Highway
Hard Surface Road
Campsite or Picknic Area
Creek or Stream

Glen Iron
Weikert
Woodward
Ingleby
Millheim
Coburn
Spring Mills
Penn's Cave
(Source of Penn's Creek)

Artificials Only
(Indicated between these points)

Poe Paddy
Picnic Area

Penn's View
(Scenic overlook)

Poe Lake
(Location of Poe
Valley State Park)

Penns Creek
Centre Co.
Pine Creek
Elk Creek
Paradise Rd.
Muddy Creek
Sinking Cr.
Penns Cr.
Poe Creek
Mifflin Co.
Poe Valley Rd.
Centre Co.
Sand Mt. Rd.
Union Co.
Snyder Co.
Mifflin Co.
Snyder Co.
Mifflin Co.

0   1/2   1   2   3
Scale in Miles

Willow arch near Spring Mills

PENN'S CREEK

---

*M*any trout streams flaunt a wide reputation. Penn's Creek's is deserved. A limestone stream with a freestone character, it boasts enough water to occupy any one angler, or group of anglers, with several lifetimes of fishing challenge and adventure. Each year thousands of anglers from a score of states and foreign countries enjoy the opportunities afforded by this magnificent waterway. Penn's is home to the most famous Green Drake hatch in the eastern United States, attendance at which is mandatory for the serious hatch-matcher (so is falling in and getting skunked during the hatch). In addition to the main stem, numerous tributaries provide even more sport. As if that were not enough, Penn's flows through pleasant surroundings, offering more to visitors than just fishing fun. The entire drainage provides a tremendous variety of recreation to a host of tourists, yet the term "tourist trap" is never heard in association with the stream or its environs.

Penn's Creek runs deeper in anglers' minds than surface appeal. It is a stream that challenges, taunts, and beckons at the same time. It can be an utter mystery, and even the best angler there, on his best day, cannot brag of having conquered Penn's. In that lies its appeal. The stream always hints at keeping something in reserve for next time—perhaps. Penn's is one of the last places where a fisherman can detect some romance in the sport.

There are other streams where I can catch more trout, although I have had some truly mind-boggling days on Penn's. There are other streams where I have better assurance of catching a big one, although the largest trout I ever saw hooked on a dry and the biggest brownie I ever saw in "open" water in Pennsylvania were at Penn's. But when I want to go fishing, in every sense of the word from anticipation to memory, I go to Penn's Creek.

A Brief Overview

Penn's Creek is divided by topography into three distinct zones, each with its own appearance and fishing characteristics. The bulk of angling interest focuses on the trout fishery in the two upper zones and the first few miles of the lower, which together total some 35 miles of stream. Angling pressure and tactics vary from one zone to another.

The upper zone comprises 13 miles—fertile agriculture basins known as Brush and Penn's Valleys. Flows, under normal conditions, consist largely of limestone springwater, running gently over a streambed of mud, sand, and gravel. Willow-lined undercuts and smooth flats support a fair population of wild brown trout, but not enough to qualify Penn's as a Pennsylvania Class A wild trout stream. Consequently, the

Covered Bridge at Millmont; they don't make 'em like this anymore!

◆

stream here is rated Class B water and receives hatchery plants shortly before and just after opening day of trout season. Early-season anglers take a heavy toll with Power Bait tactics.

The middle zone, approximately 15 miles in length, is radically different. The stream takes a rough ride through a series of gaps in a succession of high, forested ridges: the Seven Mountains. Dozens of small freestone feeders and seeps add their touch to the water's chemistry. An excellent population of wild brown trout exists in the first dozen miles, harbored by the mountains' castoff boulders that pave heavy riffles and deep pools.

The middle zone is what most anglers refer to when they talk about "fishing Penn's". It receives the heaviest pressure, for it is scenic, has excellent structure, and flaunts an unmatched range of aquatic life, making fishing there both fun and frustrating. Most of this water is rated Class A and not stocked. Anglers here are generally more skilled, because more ability is required to catch the Creator's product than man's. Most fly-fish, but alongside them can be observed the best bait men in the northeastern United States. Unfortunately, many anglers kill much, if not all of their catch.

After pushing through the hills, Penn's enters its lower zone—the pastoral Buffalo Valley. The stream is still Class A where it exits the hills, but quickly changes to Class B because of summer warming and liberal creel limits. Trout are stocked for the first few miles of Penns' passage through the Buffalo Valley, and they draw typical Pennsylvania Opening Day crowds. Wild trout are still present, however, and they, as well as the presence of good hatches, attract fly rod pressure. But when summer comes, lower Penn's is considered bass water from the village of Glen Iron all the way to its confluence with the Susquehanna River.

Geologic and Historic Background

Penn's Creek is blessed by geology and cursed by man. Nature bestowed more gifts upon its watershed than are enjoyed by most trout waters, but those same attributes also brought man, whose use of the basin resulted in problems confronting the fishery today. Despite these threats, Penn's, by

virtue of its strong backbone of natural endowments, continues to be a viable trout stream. The cardinal elements of this fishery took hundreds of millions of years to create, and a similar span of time to erode into present form. Man's activities, of much shorter duration, nonetheless play an important part in angling on Penn's Creek.

Present-day Brush, Penn's, and Buffalo Valleys are located near the center of Pennsylvania's Valley and Ridge physiographic province, a great arc of mountains running diagonally across the state from Bedford County on the Maryland border to a point near East Stroudsburg on the Delaware River. Originally the bed of a vast, shallow sea, the region was formed by intermittent collisions of the African and North American Plates, which reared the Appalachian Mountains. Peculiarities in rock strata under the leading edge of the mountains caused the uplift to ripple, in places exposing massive deposits of soluble limestone.

Water repelled from less permeable formations on either side of the limestone wore away at its surface, leaving substantial valleys flanked by long high ridges. Because of fracturing and limestone's solubility, water in large volume was admitted into the ground, often disappearing en masse through large depressions called "swallow holes". This type of terrain, known as karst, conducts groundwater to places where the land's surface meets the water table. Springs result, the water carrying with it nutrients leached from the rock it has passed through. In Brush Valley, where water from a large area is channeled underground to one spring, Penn's Creek is born.

Penn's Creek's resilient trout fishery is the result of a happy set of geologic circumstances. Foremost in importance is the influence of terrain. The watershed's mean elevation is 1,330 feet in its upper portions. At Penn's Creek's latitude, groundwater at these altitudes maintains average annual temperatures of 38-51 degrees Fahrenheit, well within the range trout need. The elevation works in concert with the natal valleys' karst topography, which stores exceptional amounts of groundwater and releases it, in constant flow, into the stream. Accordingly, Penn's suffers less of the boom/bust flow and temperature fluctuation affecting freestone streams. Barring heavy downpours, the stream is usually slow to rise. Once

◆

Exit from Penns' Cave: The source of Penn's Creek.

Penn's Creek from Penns' view.

high, it takes considerable time to drop. While temperatures can get uncomfortably high in dry summers, they do so slowly and with much less negative effect than on many other waters.

Groundwater here is of a fertility above average because of the limestone substrate. The chief minerals present, calcium carbonates, are remains of ancient life whose compressed remains form limestone. These elemental building blocks for invertebrates are present in quantity sufficient to nurture a healthy aquatic food chain. The same minerals also buffer the effects of acid precipitation and runoff from low-pH soils of the flanking ridges, and account for Penns' good pH and alkalinity, which range respectively from 7.5 to 8.2 and from 90-164, depending on flow and location.

A fascinating aspect of karst topography's effect on Penn's Creek's fishery is that almost every stream in Penn's and Brush Valleys sinks into the ground at some point. This often causes confusion as to just what is flowing where. For instance, the "official" source of Penn's, which under conventional definition of the term is to be found at the farthest point up a stream where water flows year-round, is one of several unnamed runs that trickle down hollows on the side of Nittany Mountain. These candidates all disappear into swallow holes, however, which can be found along Route 192 west of Madisonburg. The sunken rivulets flow underground to Penn's Cave, where they re-emerge at what is considered, for practical purposes, the source of Penn's Creek.

Likewise, Penns' major tributaries in its upper zone—Elk

Pine, and Sinking Creeks—also sink and run, sight unseen, through significant parts of their way. Anglers must be careful in such places; I have fallen into hidden sinks in a streambed, escaping only by luck. Another unusual fishing problem occurs in rainy weather, when water flows for miles in what are dry stream channels at other times of the year. These wet-weather waterways are, in all appearances, perfectly good trout streams, even to the point of insect hatches which develop from nymphs washed in from areas of year-round flow, as well as trout which have migrated into the ordinarily dry beds. It is possible to spend a fruitless day fishing the intermittent part of one of these watercourses while a mile or two away other anglers are enjoying good sport in permanent pools and riffles.

The creek's most negative factor is also a result of geology. Penn's is a murky stream. Some turbidity is a natural result of the water's fertility. Algae thrives in limestone water, and its constant drift often gives the water a greenish cast. Another, less healthy reason lies in valley soils, which are fine and often loose. Consequently, Penn's is easily roiled. This, too, is a naturally occurring phenomenon. But as we shall see, man has greatly aggravated the situation.

Mountains dividing the upper zone from the lower make the stream's best fishery. Much of the 554 square mile watershed consists of mountain land. In sharp contrast to the valleys, land on the ridges is thin, rocky, and infertile. Water drains easily from this landscape, coursing down steep-sided slopes and hollows. In some cases, these rills entirely disappear into swallow holes. Others, such as Poe Creek and Cherry Run, drain directly into the mainstream. The mountain water is of comparatively low pH. Where it enters the ground in the valleys it is chemically enriched by its contact with carbonate bedrock and eventually adds to the volume of springs. Elsewhere the mountain streams join directly with Penn's, contributing vital cold water.

By happy accident of the earth's ancient movements, the Seven Mountains group of the Appalachians, where most of the direct-entering little creeks on the watershed are found, are

Penn's Valley–The heart of Central Pennsylvania.

Coburn trestle.

Limestone formation in Penn's Cave: Source of the fishery's fertility.

located exactly where the cooling effect of valley springs plays out. The heights' placement is providential to the fishery. In addition to furnishing cold water, they shade the stream somewhat and the million years worth of rubble they have shed provides wonderful cover for trout. Even though water draining into Penn's from the Seven Mountains is more acidic than that of the mainstream, the stream remains predominately alkaline in chemical makeup. Character and appearance of this part of Penn's, however, resembles that of freestone streams in all aspects save clarity. This zone is the most productive and popular part of the fishery, as well as the most scenic and difficult to access.

The tributaries' effects on the fishery cannot be understated. In addition to donating cold water to the mainstream, their purity and clean gravel provide ideal spawning sites. If these little creeks did not exist, the wild trout fishery would be less productive. There would be fewer trout to stay in water that warmed quickly earlier in the year, and stayed warmer longer.

The path Penn's takes through the Seven Mountains almost defies rational thought. Thrice the water makes 180-degree turns to get around mountains. A local practical joke is to take visitors through one of the old railroad tunnels and watch bewilderment grow as they try making sense of water flowing the opposite direction of what they last saw. I have seen people so fooled as to inquire about the name of the "new" stream and where it flowed into Penn's! Other twists are less severe, but more frequent. It is seldom possible to see more than a few hundred yards up or downstream, and forest-covered hillsides overshadow anglers wherever they fish.

After escaping the Seven Mountains, Penn's enters its lower zone. The hills gradually pull back from the water, and gradient drops. Springs and seeps are common, but their volume is not large enough to alter what is now a small river. Structure is good because of large amounts of rubble washed down from the hill mass left behind, but the trout fishery peters out because of rising water temperatures. In fact, to most trout anglers, the lower reaches are just a line on a map.

As topography changes along Penn's, so do water tempera-

tures. Given normal precipitation, good trout temperatures are found, at least part of the day, anywhere in the first 25 miles and often below. But during drought years the fishery, like that of other streams, suffers. When drought hits, Penns' upper miles do a very good job of caring for their finned charges. Downstream, large areas of the mainstream will empty themselves as trout migrate to cooler havens. A thermometer can be a trout man's best friend at these times; do not waste your time in water over 70 degrees.

A drought's impact on Penns' trout is to noticeably reduce the average size of fish, with an accompanying reduction in numbers. Unfortunately, larger fish suffer the highest mortality. In compensation, there is a noticeable rebound in size during years of normal rainfall, when smaller fish grow quickly to fill vacant slots left by larger trout.

Were Penn's a typical eastern trout stream, recent dry summers endured by the Mid-Atlantic states would have dealt a terrible blow to the fishery. Penn's is made of better stuff than that, and I was never as fully aware of this than during the spring of 1994. Drought in the summer of 1993 had caused many trout to migrate, and favorite haunts in the Buffalo Valley's west end were devoid of trout that fall. So severe were conditions in the east that reports of fish kills were common, including one from New York's Beaverkill. What would 1994 bring for Penn's?

Good fishing. Populations and average size were down, but many good catches were reported, even in places lacking trout the preceding fall. In fact, I did not hear any complaints from Penn's Creek veterans, a somewhat vocal group, about num-

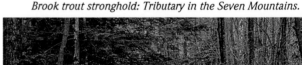

Brook trout stronghold: Tributary in the Seven Mountains.

Anglers at Paddy Mountain Tunnel.

◆

bers of trout caught. Not only did I have a couple of my best days ever on the stream, but they happened with wild trout in places where, the previous fall, I would have felt chubs or bass on the end of my line.

The secret of this fishery's resiliency under duress is simple. There are many places for trout to find cool water during hot spells and, equally important, Penn's warms slowly, giving trout time to migrate. Penns' warm-weather migration has been going on for years, and has been noted by famous anglers such as George Harvey and Charles Wetzel, both of whom were aware of the movements impact on fishing.

It would be difficult to create a better trout river the size of Penn's. Every terrain feature along the stream seems to have been placed with the express purpose of sustaining an exceptional fishery. Unfortunately, man's role in the watershed has detracted from this splendid waterway.

Penn's Creek prior to the arrival of Europeans was part of a stately, magnificent ecosystem, the like of which the world will never see again. Hemlock and white pine packed the ridges so densely that even the Indians shunned them, for the natural monoculture did not lend itself to a diversity of wildlife. Snow lingered so long in the permanent twilight of the great trees' shade that uplands were often impassable until May, and early white settlers called these regions "Shades of Death". Valley floors had more variety of trees and animals, often opening up into prairies that offered easier travel and fertile, easily tilled soils, attributes that led to their being the focus of Indian and European development.

White settlers arrived in the watershed during one of the most turbulent times of North American history. The Susquehannock Tribe, which had inhabited the basin of the river that now bears their name, had been defeated in fur trade wars of the late Seventeenth Century. To fill the vacuum left by their demise, the Iroquois Confederacy, whose lands lay to the north, imported displaced Indians from as far away as North Carolina. The Iroquois hoped the refugees would become grateful allies and act as a buffer against European colonization.

The Delawares were one of the tribes welcomed into the region by the Iroquois. They had, by 1750, sold their land in eastern Pennsylvania to William Penn's colony and migrated to the Susquehanna basin. As Pennsylvania expanded and purchased more land, it became inevitable that friction would arise, especially when deeds were misunderstood on either side. The willingness of white settlers to ignore purchase boundaries exacerbated the situation, and with the outbreak of the French and Indian War, force became the arbiter of who owned what.

Penn's Creek was at the center of this turmoil. In 1754 most of the land encompassing the stream was purchased, by which time settlers had already pushed some ten miles up the creek from the Susquehanna. Further expansion came to a bloody halt when Indian passions, already inflamed by Pennsylvania's interpretation of the deed of 1754 as including much more land than the Indians had intended, were further fanned by the appearance of squatters on the lower part of the stream.

In 1755, General Edward Braddock's defeat near the forks of the Ohio placed all of Pennsylvania in grave danger. Emboldened by the disaster, a band of Indians under Delaware Chief Keckenipaulin fell on isolated settlements in the Buffalo Valley near New Berlin and wiped them out. Twenty five settlers were killed or taken prisoner, and so great a fear spread that by the end of the year no settlers remained in the watershed.

Fortunately, the Indians did not follow up their victory, even though aided with French arms and men. Their lack of initiative was a major strategic blunder, because there was little to oppose them. So strong was the Indian position in 1758 that Pennsylvania signed a new deed relinquishing claim to some of the lands listed in the deed of 1754, sparing eastern Pennsylvania an assault that could have pushed the English into the Delaware River. After years of terror, land purchases and settlement resumed after the conclusion of the French and Indian War in 1763.

It was during this time that Penn's Creek was named. The deed of 1754 lists it under its Indian name, Kaarondinhah, the meaning of which is lost. Early settlers and maps labeled it "Mahany", "Big Mahany", "Big Mahanoy", and "Mahoning" Creeks, terms used to denote deer and elk licks. It was named John Penn's Creek in the deed of 1758, after William Penn's grandson, under whose auspices the original purchase was made. Today it is called Penn's Creek, or simply Penn's.

The end of the French and Indian War encouraged reoccupation of lands deserted for almost ten years. The first recorded description of the upper basin was made in 1764 by James Potter, an energetic Pennsylvania militia captain. Potter and a companion traveled up the West Branch of the Susquehanna, Bald Eagle and Spring Creeks to the location of present-day Bellefonte, and climbed Nittany Mountain. Near the future town of Centre Hall they beheld Penn's Valley. "By Heavens,

Thompson, I have discovered an empire!" are the words legend has Potter utter, the first white man to see what is still an inspiring view.

Potter and Thompson descended into the valley and camped near today's crossroads of Routes 45 and 144, where they found a spring. It is well they had plenty of water, because their food consisted of what they could scrape from an old beaver hide! Fortified with this unappetizing fare, the two companions then exited Penn's Valley by following Penn's Creek, and ended up back at the Susquehanna near Selinsgrove. Potter was enthusiastic about his find, and filed claim to a large part of Penn's Valley, a portion of which, Potter Township, is named after him.

Parts of the watershed left in Indian hands were purchased by Pennsylvania in 1768, after which settlement of the upper drainage began. James Potter returned to farm the valley he had discovered, just in time to endure frontier upheavals that occurred during the American Revolution. Indian massacres in Pennsylvania's Appalachian region caused settlers to flee in what became known as "The Great Runaway". Penn's Valley was abandoned after several people were killed; no whites lived there between 1780 and 1784.

Indian Wars continued to plague Pennsylvania until 1795, but Penn's Creek was spared further depredation. The history of the watershed after this time is an American success story of frontier development, but it changed water quality in Penn's forever.

Mountain land in the drainage was little settled by immigrants, but the valleys quickly filled. Agriculture became, and remains, the chief industry of the watershed. Fertile soils and gentle contours make Penn's, Brush, and Buffalo Valleys some of the world's most productive farmland, and adequate rainfall renders irrigation unnecessary. But the same rains wash large amounts of farm silt into the stream, and Penn's is widely known as "the first to get muddy and the last to clear". This often affects the plans of those who fish Penn's Creek today. Many calls are logged at Flyfisher's Paradise fly shop inquiring about Penn's clarity, and answers often depend on what part of the agricultural year is in progress. Anglers familiar with the problem travel to the area with alternative streams in mind should Penn's be muddy. "Penn's Creek was always a muddy stream when I started fishing it in the forties, and it still is today." (Joe Humphreys)

To open up Penns' upper basin for communication and commerce, a road was commissioned in 1773, "...to run from the east end of the Great Plains (as that part of Penn's Valley near Old Fort was known) to Sunbury." (*Linn's History of Centre and Clinton Counties*) This was the forerunner of Route 45, which thousands of anglers use to access the drainage.

Despite the existence of a road, early settlers found it easier to use Penn's for transporting farm products to markets in the Susquehanna Valley. During high water "arks" would ride

The bad news: Penn's after a rain.

Streamside trail in spring.

◆

the current, most making the trip safely. One that did not was loaded with butter, and smashed onto ledges behind Little Mountain in Union County. These rocks are known to this day as "The Butter Rocks" among local fishermen.

A side effect of agriculture was the use of the stream for milling grain. Mill dams on Penn's blocked the stream and raised water temperatures. Many of these dams are gone, but those that remain, like the Penn's Creek Feed Mills dam upstream from Coburn, negatively impact the fishery.

Other dams were erected to trap migrating eels. Prior to the erection of power dams on the lower Susquehanna, which barred most eels from their traditional range throughout the big river's basin, the catadromous fish were numerous in Penn's. Eels today are few, but occasionally one is seen. The old "eel walls" have fallen into disrepair, but their remnants, like the one at Stillhouse Hollow below Coburn, add interesting structure to the stream.

Nineteenth Century development in the United States featured the building of railroads into every possible market. In 1853, the Lewisburg, Centre, and Spruce Creek Railroad was founded to serve Buffalo, Penn's, and Nittany Valleys, as well as connecting them with larger valleys east and west. Construction proceeded intermittently, and by completion late in the century, the railroad had changed hands and name, becoming the Lewisburg and Tyrone Railroad. The railroad is now defunct, but its path negotiated the water gap between

Penn's and Buffalo Valleys, and the old bed remains the most convenient way to access much of Penns' best water.

The railroad opened up the region for great logging drives that denuded area mountains around the turn of the century. Earlier, Seven Mountain forests had escaped the woodsmen's axes for lack of ready transport, because most streams in the region were too small to float logs. The laying down of a main line solved the lumbermen's problem. Boom towns sprang up, and logging tramways pushed into almost every mountain hollow. But in a twenty year span, ending about 1905, the trees

◆

Some Ful-O-Pep gets into the trout.

15

Sturdy Pennsylvania farmers built sturdy barns.

♦

were exhausted and the boom went bust.

There is little evidence left of the most intense human activity ever seen in the mountains surrounding Penn's. At the mouth of Poe Creek, where the logging town of Poe Mills once sheltered 300 souls, there is now only a quiet public campground and some sportsmen's camps. No sound of sawmill or steam engine breaks the morning quiet; there are no permanent residents. Obvious reminders of logging are the little tramways' old roadbeds, which are less evident with each passing year. Even when overgrown, the old grades often remain the best way to get from one place to another in the hills, and I often use them on fishing jaunts.

The echoes of axe and saw died over a shattered landscape, and Penn's Creek's fishery suffered ecological disaster. Loss of shade and erosion in the lumberjacks' wake played havoc with water quality. Freestone tributaries were hardest hit, because they do not have the resilience of limestone streams. In time, a new forest grew, but it is predominately hardwood, which gives up less water to springs and streams than did the original conifers.

We are fortunate to have the hardwoods. In the early part of the Twentieth Century, Pennsylvania created its State Forest System, an act of incredible foresight. Each year benefits of this wise conservation effort are enjoyed by millions of people. Thousands of acres of Penns' watershed were protected in the Bald Eagle and Rothrock State Forests. State Parks and State Picnic areas were later added to the system, including Poe Valley and Poe Paddy Campgrounds, popular campgrounds for Penn's anglers.

Demand for recreational opportunities led to construction of two dams on the watershed, neither of which has been good for Penn's Creek. In 1937 Poe Valley Lake was formed by damming Poe Creek, ruining an excellent wild brook trout fishery through thermal pollution. Further, the dam is periodically drawn down and poisoned to eliminate rough fish, and on one occasion the poison got out of control and killed trout for a long distance downstream. Colyer Lake was created in 1966 by damming Sinking Creek. Like the dam on Poe Creek, the one on Sinking Creek ruined a brook trout fishery. But Colyer Lake's effects on Penn's are less than those of Poe Valley's, because Sinking Creek sinks a few miles below the lake, and cools considerably before resurging to join Penns.

Penn's Creek's story is one of an excellent natural resource struggling to maintain integrity in the face of man's degradation. Fortunately, two hundred years of human activity have not yet erased two hundred million years of nature's.

Angling History

Penn's Creek's angling history is not unlike other eastern trout fisheries. Where water temperatures permitted, the watershed supported brook trout until the early part of the Twentieth Century, the native char abounding in both main stem and tributaries. With logging and resultant gradual warming of the watershed, the brookies' range shrank. Wild brook

16

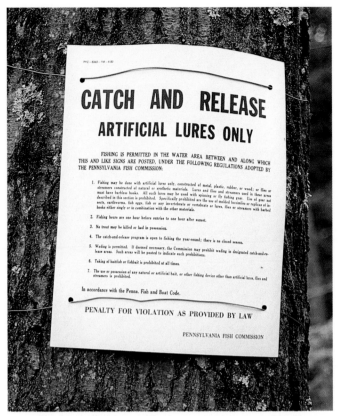

The kind of sign we like to see near a trout stream.

◆

trout are numerous today only in some feeders, although occasionally one shows up in the mainstream. Brook trout held out for a while near Spring Mills, and I used to catch many there in the mid-seventies, but their time in Penn's Creek is sadly vanished.

Memories of old-time fishing on Penn's Creek are buried with the early fishermen in little graveyards of the region. The oldest record I have are boyhood recollections of the tales of my grandfather, Paul Kramer, a native of Penn's Valley who fished local waters from just before the turn of the century. At that time fly fishing was not done, being considered an inefficient means of transporting trout from water to table. Anything went, from alder switch with string and worm to trot lines set out at night. Papa's most memorable trout from that era was a big one taken in tributary Pine Creek, on a rod left unattended (times have changed!) while he went to a nearby store for groceries.

Brown trout saved the day, as they did on many other waters, but the exact date of their introduction is a mystery. Early stockings of the import were often made by individuals who had been given fingerlings by the Pennsylvania Fish Commission. Records were kept of who received trout, but not where they were released. It is probable that by the time Penn's received its earliest recorded official stocking of browns in 1931, the newcomers had already established themselves. Penn's Creek played good host to the first plants; their wild descendants are the backbone of today's fishery.

Fishing on Penn's remained relatively unchanged, and

undiscovered, through the first half of the Twentieth Century. "A few people fished the stream then, but not very many. You could look up and down the stream and not see much competition; pressure was primarily from local anglers." (Joe Humphreys, reminiscing about the forties.) His words about times past are echoed by his friend and mentor, George Harvey, "You could have the stream almost to yourself, anytime, and almost any stretch."

Most fishermen at that time fished bait, with few flyrodders in evidence, and prisoners taken were not released. "...they used to call it the "Mosquito Hole", and one of the Kerstetters lived along there. He was a minnow fisherman, and I used to stop and talk to him. He had a wire net screen in the stream there, about 10 foot square. He used to catch big fish and keep them alive in there. I went down one time, and he had about ten or twelve trout in that screen that were all in the 20-inch class or bigger, all taken in one week." (George Harvey) "Locals were the best group of fishermen on the stream. Old Les Rote used to carry a tank on his back, with a shoulder harness. He'd fish daily, and he knew where the big fish were, and he'd fish a spot, make a few casts, jump in the car, and drive to the next spot. The reason he carried that tank, he had a spring hole somewhere. He'd keep the fish alive in the tank until he got them to the spring hole, keep the fish in there, and when somebody wanted a big fish, he'd sell it to him." (Joe Humphreys)

It was not until after World War II that Penn's became widely known. Prior American angling literature had focused on Adirondack, Catskill, and Pocono waters, which were bathed in limelight by their literate clientele. Publicity awarded to Central Pennsylvania streams centered mostly on northern tier freestoners and on Spring Creek, where Fisherman's Paradise garnered an international reputation. Penn's Creek enjoyed benign neglect, primarily because its location and lack of accommodations made it inconvenient to fish under conditions of the times.

Penn's did have one resident angling author, Charles Wetzel, who kept a small house at Glen Iron. Wetzel, the

◆

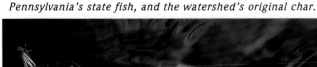

Pennsylvania's state fish, and the watershed's original char.

The backbone of the fishery: Wild brown trout.

Typical opening weekend: Crowded stream, high water.

◆

author of *Trout Flies—Naturals and Imitations*, *Practical Fly Fishing*, and *The Art of Fly Tying*, had a roving foot. He did not fish or write about Penn's exclusively or excessively. Excerpts from his diary are a wonderful legacy of Pennsylvania fly fishing in the middle part of the Twentieth Century. According to dean of American fly fishing George Harvey, who fished with Wetzel in the forties and fifties, "Charlie Wetzel was a good fisherman, and he had a reputation of being one of the better fly fishermen of his time." That is an endorsement of the first order.

Penns' lack of notoriety changed dramatically with the publication, in the April 7, 1958 edition of *Sports Illustrated*, of an article by Sparse Grey Hackle, AKA Alfred Miller. The late Sparse, a venerated figure of American fly fishing, had paid a visit to Penn's and was impressed by the water and its potential. His glowing account of the stream finished with "...there is no fishing in the East to compare with that on Penn's Creek."

Sparse's article hit the newsstands just before Pennsylvania's Opening Day of trout season, and elicited a response from anglers similar to that one would get by rolling a wine bottle into a flophouse. An army of eager fishermen invaded the watershed, all fired up to get in on the action. Penn's was changed forever in the angling gold rush that followed. "That's when you started to get an influx of fishermen from all around, and they'd come from New York and other places to fish Penn's Creek because the way he (Sparse) wrote the article. You'd be surprised at how fast it (the crowd) grew, because everyone that came to fish told somebody else about it." (George Harvey)

Fishing camps proliferated, populated by anglers from all parts of Pennsylvania. The burgeoning streamside crowd was further swelled by travelers from other states, who arrived in increasing numbers as postwar road construction eased travel.

The numbers of new fishermen, as well as their behavior, was discouraging to Penn's Creek veterans. "...the fellows didn't know what etiquette was along the stream. They'd come right up. I've been fishing and casting to a rising trout and had somebody come down and cast over the same fish. The first place that ever happened to me was on Penn's Creek. I lost interest in it because there were so many fishermen there. You couldn't find a place to fish." (George Harvey)

Another profound change to the fishing on Penn's had started after World War II, with the advent of spinning tackle. Anglers previously baffled with skills necessary to fish fly or bait tackle could now reach any water on the stream with inexpensive, easy to use gear. A child could use spinning tackle, and millions did. This trend, coupled with the now-infamous article, resulted in overharvest on Penn's. "At one time, there were more fish, no doubt about it. But as time went on they were depleted. Go down (to Penn's) now...if you take one 20-inch fish you're doing a great job. There just aren't that many big fish left." (Joe Humphreys) "The fishing before the Sparse Grey Hackle article was fantastic, and the number of trout in the 12-16-inch range was fantastic." (George Harvey)

Current Pennsylvania Fish and Boat Commission survey data supports Joe and George. Numbers of fish are excellent, but the average size of Penn's Creek trout is smaller now, with

20

8-12 inches being the norm. Twenty-inchers are present but uncommon, only one or two turning up in a 300-meter survey section. The largest fly-caught trout I've seen taken from Penn's was a 24-incher caught in Union County by David Carson of Boalsburg, Centre County.

After "the article", Penn's Creek had much more print attached to its name, chiefly by Pennsylvania authors. Vince Marinaro and Charles Fox made regular Green Drake pilgrimages, but they did not patronize Penn's exclusively among the many fine waters in Pennsylvania's northern limestone region. Another famous Cumberland Valley flyrodder, Ed Shenk, became familiar with the stream while working with the U.S. Geologic Survey. The most prolific writer has been Charles Meck, whose *Meeting and Fishing the Hatches* and *Pennsylvania Trout Streams and Their Hatches* have done considerable work in listing the hatches of Penn's. "Charlie" joined forces with Gregory Hoover, an aquatic entomologist at nearby Penn State University. They collaborated to write *Great Rivers, Great Hatches*, a book highlighting many of America's best trout rivers, including Penn's. Greg's master's thesis studied Penns' Green Drake, and his encyclopedic knowledge of aquatic insects and teaching abilities make him a demand figure on the fly fishing lecture circuit. Penn's has also made every statewide guide to Pennsylvania trout fishing I have seen, the most notable of which are *Pennsylvania Trout and Salmon Guide*, by Mike Sajna, and *Trout Streams of Pennsylvania*, by Dwight Landis.

Well known non-residents have also made contributions. Al Caucci and Bob Nastasi made several trips to Penn's while gathering data for their book *Hatches*, and Ernest Schwiebert

◆

George Harvey: The master.

also visited the stream, where he interviewed Charles Wetzel for an article that appeared in *Fly Fisherman* Magazine.

Ironically, the best known Pennsylvanians who frequent Penn's Creek, George Harvey and Joe Humphreys, have done little to publicize the stream. Instead, George's *Techniques of Trout Fishing and Fly Tying*, and Joe's *On the Trout Stream with Joe Humphreys* and *Joe Humphreys's Trout Tactics*, along with Joe's videos "Nymphing Strategy" and "Dry Fly Strategy" have focused on angling technique, and are regarded as gospel by many flyrodders. For a span of 53 years the two men taught accredited fly fishing and casting courses at Penn State, the first such offered anywhere. Begun by George, who upon retirement had taught a total of over 24,000 people, the classes were continued in 1970 by Joe, who taught thousands more. Both men are now retired, but the Angling Class recently celebrated its 60th year in the capable hands of Vance McCullough.

George and Joe learned to adapt flies and methods to Penn's. Because the stream is such a hard taskmaster, what they developed there worked well on other, less demanding waters. Both men developed successful Green Drake patterns as a result of their experience on Penn's. Joe credits the stream and his fishing buddies there with helping him perfect nymphing skills, which stood him in good stead when representing the United States in international fly fishing competitions. "Lewie (Weaver) was the guy who got me into the mono technique. He fished with Les Rote, Butch Kerstetter, and the Kerstetter boys. As soon as monofilament came out, they didn't want to buy the fancy reels. They loaded mono on the automatic reels, and used their fly rods, and strung live minnows. And used so many shot, it looked like a rosary. And they would heave those rigs out, and work them with both hands. They would really churn the bottom, and take fish like crazy. But I didn't like to fish live bait, and I wanted to be a flyfisher. But one day I just switched from live bait to (artificial) nymphs, and started to take fish that I could never get to before. And so this is how I got into running deep water. We started that in 1949." (Joe Humphreys)

The last few decades of the Twentieth Century have brought more changes to the fishing on Penn's. Adding to angling pressure was the decline of nearby Spring Creek. Expansion at Penn State University and attendant development in State College have wrought fearful havoc on what was formerly one of the world's most famous trout streams. With the demise of insect hatches there, including the extinction of its Green Drake hatch, not to mention the ban on eating pesticide-contaminated fish from the waterway, local and visiting anglers sought other opportunities. Penn's picked up some of the heat. Additionally, management of Penns' fishery has altered since the inception of the Pennsylvania Fish and Boat Commission's Operation Future in 1981.

The watershed used to be so intensively stocked that streams as small as two or three feet wide received hatchery trout. One such trickle was too small to appear on topographic maps! Much less stocking is now done under management guidelines that place more emphasis on wild trout. Much of Penn's, as well as most of the smaller creeks, are no longer stocked. With the exception of Poe Valley Lake, fewer fish are planted less often in those places still stocked.

After a couple of attempts at establishing special regulations areas in the fifties and sixties, an "Artificials Only, Catch and Release" section was firmly established in 1976, making Penn's even more appealing to flyfishers. Credit for the establishment of the project is largely due to the efforts of streamside landowners, who worked tirelessly to create the project. David Johnson, Malcolm Farrow, and William Lewis deserve our deepest appreciation for their efforts. To their water was added the Raymond Winter tract, which was purchased by the (then) Pennsylvania Fish Commission. The new special regulations water quickly became a favorite destination for flyrodders from all over the east.

These changes, along with broader trends among fishermen, have resulted in a different angling crowd. Throngs of fish truck followers used to be a common sight from mid-April through June. Because of stocking cutbacks, fish truck crowds are only in evidence from Spring Mills to Coburn and in the Union County portions of the mainstream. Mercifully, pressure created by the hatchery plants is now of shorter duration, making more elbow room available for dedicated sportsmen. Genuinely proficient bait fishermen are declining in number, too. These men know the stream and understand trout, as well as how to effectively use a variety of natural baits. I have seen them key on events that lend themselves to the use of bait in the same way that flyrodders follow hatches, and it is a rare day (or night) that there are not a few of these highly skilled anglers somewhere on the watershed. Younger fishermen are not being recruited to replace those who retire because of the effort involved to follow this angling path, which requires as much skill as fly fishing.

Until recently, typical Penn's flyfishers fished wet flies with the old down-and-across method, unless a hatch brought fish to the surface, when large traditional dries were employed. An amusing note to that effect is found in Vince Marinaro's limestone masterpiece, A Modern Dry Fly Code, where a Union County angler is quoted "...no one in that district used anything smaller than a size 14 in dry flies." These days, anything goes. On one recent foray to the stream, I witnessed anglers loaded with state-of-the-art gear casting emergers, caddis dries, sulfur spinners, and comparaduns to trout rising in one of Penn's hemlock-shaded pools. A couple of elderly wet fly and streamer fishermen were worked over the head of the pool, and a nymph fisher plied the riffle upstream. To a long-time observer of Penn's fishing, the activity is interesting. "Penn's Creek offers a fascinating mix of both old and new in fly fishing. It is one of the few waters in the area where you can still see old time wet fly techniques in use. At the same time there are some very innovative anglers fishing the stream." (Steve Sywensky)

The credit for Penn's Creek's angling tradition is entirely

The witching hour.

This one has a chance to grow under new regulations.

◆

due to the stream and its trout. Its varied water, complex food chain, and wild browns make fishing there challenging, and fishermen had to rise to the occasion. In doing so, they became better anglers. "The average fisherman on Penn's Creek is a cut above the rest." (Joe Humphreys)

A Closer Look at the Layout of Penn's Creek

Few streams make as dramatic an entry into the world as Penn's Creek, emerging as it does from Penn's Cave, a water cavern large enough to permit boating inside the very bowels of the earth. Here is the end result of water seeping into many square miles of land, gathered together, and expelled in one place by the karst terrain. Where it first sees daylight, Penn's is small in size but already rich in nutrients gathered from rock eroded by the hidden stream far underground.

Penn's Creek's first four miles are typical of a pure Pennsylvania spring creek. It flows with a gentle, even clip, leaving its Brush Valley birthplace by skirting the end of Brush Mountain, at which point it enters Penn's Valley. These first miles are a continuous succession of slight riffles and small pools, seldom more than 20 feet wide. Surroundings are pastoral: cows, cornfields, and small woodlots follow closely upon each other. Little volume is added to the stream, save what the occasional small spring or seep contributes.

Right away the stream holds trout, which swim even in

the cavern itself. Some stocking is done at the cave for tourists to view, but an excellent population of wild browns exists from the source downstream to Spring Mills. Unfortunately, almost all of this water is posted because of past thoughtless acts of "sportsmen".

Aquatic life here is already surprisingly diverse. Sulfurs, Blue-winged Olives, and the tan caddis so widespread in Pennsylvania are the best aquatic hatches in this portion of Penn's, but March Browns and other large flies are also present. Green Drakes are not found on this part of Penn's, but there is a fair Trico hatch. Perhaps the best fishing on this part of Penn's is with terrestrials in the summer.

Penn's Creek is like a child in the farms of its upper reaches, but it quickly matures at Spring Mills. Here, the stream's size doubles with large upwellings of springwater and the influx of Sinking Creek, its first major tributary. Penn's leaves town much larger, now averaging 30-50 feet across.

Penn's Creek is a classic farm-country stream as it wends its way across Penn's Valley. Undercut banks lined with willows and logjams are predominant stream features. Riffles are few and short, the water favoring a more dignified pace. Aptly-named Muddy Creek enters Penn's a couple of miles below Spring Mills, but its small flow adds little volume and does not alter the stream's character. The tranquil glides continue for a total of five miles below Spring Mills, where the water's even flow expires into a long millpond formed by the Penn's Creek

Feed Mills' dam.

This stretch is champion dry fly water, especially with ter-restrials. The springs in Spring Mills also make this the best part of Penn's temperature-wise. This could be a prime spring creek fishery, but it suffers tremendously from farm runoff and fishing pressure. The muddy streambed is not good holding water, and spawning is hindered. Consequently, while there is a fair wild trout population, it is not as good as rockier stretch-es. The smooth bottom is easy to wade, a different story from the lively conditions farther downstream.

Most of this stretch is open to public fishing, and is stocked pre- and in-season. Pressure from opening day through June is constant, often heavy. Large numbers of trout are removed under generous creel limits, and this hurts the resource considerably. Average size of the survivors is 6-12-inches, with the occasional larger brown coming to net. The Fish and Boat Commission monitors this part of Penn's, and is keeping an open mind to possible future changes.

When Penn's leaves the dam, it no longer meanders through the countryside. Instead, the stream adopts a purpose-ful straight course toward a gap in the Seven Mountains at the sleepy hamlet of Coburn. The path is dictated by the base of First Mountain, and along this picturesque ridge the stream flows. The water's pace quickens, and the streambed contains more rubble. Just above the little town, and eleven miles from its natal spring, Penn's slows for a short stretch, as if tarrying for a last look at familiar, well-loved surroundings.

The two miles of water between the Feed Mills' dam and Coburn are much warmer than the stream above the dam. On hot days the mill pool's outflow will be at least four degrees warmer than inflow. There is a tradeoff: the dam traps some of the silt washed in from farms upstream. As a result, hatches below the dam are better in quantity and diversity than those above. Grannom caddis are present, and this is the farthest up Penn's that you will see Green Drakes.

Fishing pressure here is fierce. Because of the low density of wild trout, this section of Penn's is stocked. The hatchery trout draw crowds, with all their "gotta get my share" mentali-ty. At the close of one fine May evening on this stretch, my friend Joe Blanda and I saw a flyfisher decked out with neo-prenes, graphite, and fancy vest—carrying a chain stringer upon which some forlorn trout flapped their last. Anglers' access is rendered easy by the Penn's Creek Road, which paral-lels the water. The streambed here is easily waded, and the water is made to order for wet and dry fly tactics.

Coburn marks the most profound change in the course and volume of Penn's Creek. Here, the stream makes an abrupt, right-hand turn and charges into its water gap. As it does, its size is enlarged considerably by the influx of the combined flow of two tributaries, Elk and Pine Creeks, which have joined themselves only a half mile above their confluence with Penn's. Penn's is a full-fledged adult now, and it takes an adult to wade

◆

Logjam at Poe Paddy trestle–The local sense of humor shows.

Fanged beauty of Penn's: Watch where you step!

it. The bottom of the stream is paved with rocks and boulders from the mountains that crowd closely upon it.

With the radical change in water character comes a change in stream life. The variety of water types, ranging from surging runs through pocket water to long, slow pools, harbors an extensive food chain. No other stream in my experience holds such an amazing menu of fishable hatches than does Penn's in the 20 miles downstream from Coburn. As we shall see, this part of Penn's is renowned for taxing flyrodders' skills in tactics and pattern choice.

Angling pressure is quite heavy in Penn's middle zone, although the size of the stream, 30-110 feet in width, allows fishermen to spread out and interfere with each other less than in the smaller water above Coburn. With the exception of Green Drake time, when it is hard to find a parking space, it is usually possible to find some elbow room. Fishing here should get better in the next few years; almost eight miles from Coburn downstream to the upper end of the "Artificials Only" section has been recently designated "trophy trout" water, which restricts harvest to two trout per day over 14-inches.

There is not a continuous access road along Penn's in this mileage. Instead, roads lead to the creek at several widely spaced points, give access to a short stretch or parking area, and then either dead end or go sway from the stream. As a result, anglers drive as close as possible, and then follow either the old railroad grade, a camp driveway, or fisherman's path to the water. Fishermen in this part of Penn's do a lot of hiking.

Immediately below Coburn is one of the most easily accessed parts of Penns' middle zone. A road parallels the water for more than a mile and a half, and proximity to Route 45 makes this area the most heavily fished stretch of Penns' mountainous section. Despite the pressure, this stretch often provides fine sport. Water temperatures hold up well except during afternoons in the worst extremes of summer, and hatches are prolific. There is an excellent assortment of riffles, pocket water, runs and pools, some of which, like the pool at Tunnel Mountain, are quite impressive. There is usually activity worth pursuing here, but because of the pressure, the trout can be incredibly finicky and hard to catch. On one recent early July evening, the stream was sullen, yielding no helpful clues. Few flies were about, and in an hour-and-a-half only a few fish rose. I had to cycle through four different tactics and six fly patterns to hook nine trout. It is indicative of fishing here that I felt good about the score, considering the time of year.

The access road below Coburn ends at a parking lot beside an old railroad trestle, now maintained for foot traffic. There are some good pools just up and down from the bridge, and their denizens will test any angler's skill. Downstream from the lower pool, Penn's breaks into a long stretch of riffles, broken here and there by an occasional shallow run or short glide. This is not big fish water, but smaller ones are here in plenty, and

Action at Rainbow Riffle in the Project Water.

Grannom caddis clustering on a rock.

◆

insect hatches are often profuse. The riffles end in a series of pools that spread upstream and down from the next access point at Ingleby.

Ingleby is a small collection of camps reached by driving a mountain road from Pine Creek. There is a lot of flat water in this stretch, and it is heavily fished by dry fly addicts. Wet fly men are also here in number; this locale is one of the few places you can still see fly fishing done in the old style. I recall one veteran I saw there, a man bent almost double with years, leaning on his staff as he swung his flies down and across as he had no doubt done in the spring of his youth.

Below Ingleby, the stream shallows out for a short spell, and then makes a sharp turn that signals the beginning of its most dramatic maneuvers through the Seven Mountains. Pushing east, south, west, and then south and east again, Penn's acts as if madly seeking exit from a maze. This is fine, heavy water, strewn with boulders, the rush of water at times spreading into a majestic pool. The rugged journey continues for several miles, twisting around Slide and Paddy Mountains, and passing Poe Paddy campground, the best access point for this stretch. Poe, Panther, and Swift Runs enter in succession, adding to Penns' volume. Hatches are excellent, and due to the exceptional holding water, so is the trout population. The

water's quality is apparent, and anglers from all over the east fish here.

This is beautiful country, and its aesthetics add to the fishing experience. Mountains, trees, and water surround anglers. Wildlife abounds, with deer, bear, smaller animals, and birds much in evidence. The bear often cause a ruckus in the campgrounds. On one occasion, Ohio angler Ron Woodcock left the phone dangling from a booth when his call home was interrupted by a bruin's sudden appearance beside him. His wife, who was on the other end, was quite agitated until contact was re-established: hearing your spouse say, "Ohhh ——, there's a bear here!", and then silence, would keep anyone awake at night! Rattlesnakes are also common; and every year several anglers report close encounters with them.

For flyfishers, the lower part of the middle zone contains one of the most important parts of Penn's. A half mile below the mouth of Swift Run, midway down a boisterous rapid, the creek is crossed by a wire designating the upper boundary of the "Artificials Only" management area. Almost four miles of stream are included in this portion, and it is all splendid water. Pools are grand, fast water is magnificent. Fishing here can be the best the stream has to offer, because of catch-and-release regulations.

This is popular water, well known to eastern flyfishers. Prime reasons for its drawing power are that it offers Penns' best dry fly fishing and average size of trout. Catch-and-release ensures both. I experienced the difference between this stretch and "open" water one mid-May day. The weather was warm and overcast, excellent conditions for daytime action at this time of year, and I started fishing near Weikert, downstream from the "Artificials Only" section. A constant stream of mayflies and caddis emerged, and trout were biting—on the bottom. I had good action on March Brown nymphs, landing quite a few wild browns up to 13-inches, but did not see one trout rise in over two hours. The day already a success, I became curious about activity elsewhere on the stream. The "Artificials Only" section was a short distance away, so I motored over. I was greeted by the same stream of bugs—and rings on the water. Jerry Stercho of Lewisburg was fishing there, and took a fine brown on a dry as I came down the bank. He informed me that the surface activity had been going on for some time. I lost no time in heading for a couple of favorite spots and was rewarded, not only with trout on dries, but fish larger than those I had been catching outside of the project.

If I were allotted one last day to fish, and could choose time and place, I would spend it on the "Artificials Only" portion of Penn's Creek during the third week of May. One day spent on this water, with its wonderful variety of water types and beautiful scenery, is worth more to me than several days anywhere else. Water temperatures are optimum in late May, and hatches are at their height then. I would choose a weekday, because good fishing does not go unnoticed, and sometimes the water is well occupied with eager flyrodders.

The "Artificials Only" section is accessed from its ends. The upper end is reached by walking across the old railroad bridge upstream from Poe Paddy and then following the road bed through the Paddy Mountain tunnel and beyond. A sign beside the grade designates the upper boundary. The Penn's Creek Road parallels the lower mile-and-a-half of the project, ending at a fisherman's parking lot. There is not a continuous road that accesses the entire stretch, but the old railroad bed serves as a convenient trail.

Now for the bad news. Midway through the project water is a temperature "break point". In drought years, the lower half of the project will see many of its trout move out in mid-summer. Fortunately, they do not have far to go, in most cases traveling no more than a few hundred yards to the nearest seep or small feeder. Trout in the upper part will migrate, too, but not as much. The migration can slow fishing considerably, but cool, rainy days in any summer see first-rate action for those lucky enough to be on stream.

Penn's Creek exits the "Artificials Only" section a few miles upstream from the town of Weikert. Temperature plays an increasingly important role in fishing from this point down. As the valley widens, sources of cold water become progressively fewer, until Penn's ceases to be trout water for practical purposes. Nonetheless, this mileage is still an excellent early-season fishery, and cold spots in the stream offer opportunities even in the hottest months. Stocking resumes below the "Artificials Only" section, with pre- and in-season plantings drawing anglers from far and wide. Some large trout live in this section of Penn's, well fed by the incredible amount of feed available to them. Hatches are first-rate, and include all of the bugs found elsewhere on Penn's, as well as great quantities of baitfish, hellgrammites, and crawfish. The size of the water, up to 120 feet in width, its volume, and tough wading all conspire to make fishing as difficult as anywhere on the stream. Access to Penn's in the Buffalo Valley is similar to that in the more mountainous part of Penn's. Fishermen must drive to a point on or near the stream, and then walk.

Penns' character alters notably a couple of miles below Weikert. The stream broadens and flattens out, mirroring the valley in which it flows. Rapids are few and far between, although a good riffle/pool ratio is maintained. Fewer wild trout make their homes here, and the trout fishery is largely put-and-take down to the Route 235 bridge at Glen Iron, where stocking and practical trout fishing ceases. Penn's cannot be entirely discounted as a trout fishery, however, even in what looks more like bass water than a trout stream. Every year large wild and holdover trout are taken from this section, and aquatic life is even more abundant than upstream.

Fly Fishing on Penn's Creek: What are they taking?

Few streams rival Penn's Creek for diversity of aquatic organisms, which cover the spectrum of taxonomic orders familiar to flyfishers worldwide. This profusion became apparent to me when I participated in an effort to reestablish the Green Drake hatch on nearby Spring Creek, where the insect formerly emerged in great abundance. Members of the Spring Creek Chapter of Trout Unlimited gathered nymphs from

Penn's has a good variety of water.

Penn's by dislodging rocks and silt and seining the result. Although many of the target species were collected, they were far outnumbered by the mass of other organisms swept into the netting. Individual passes of the seine often captured several ounces of feed. The bulk of the weight was represented by large food forms such as crayfish and sculpins, but a myriad of insects ranging from midge larvae to Pteronarcys stoneflies were also brought to light, with each netful turning up at least a dozen species. While unsuccessful in its goal of transplanting the Green Drake, the attempt was startling in its revelation of just what lives in Penn's.

The total of trout stream insect species runs into the hundreds. According to Penn State entomologist Greg Hoover, there are few major eastern mayflies of which Penn's does not have at least a trace population. In addition, over 1,000 species of caddisflies, stoneflies, midges, crane flies, black flies, etc. are also present. Add to that large and small crustaceans and baitfish, as well as terrestrials and more esoteric items such as sucker eggs and aquatic worms, and you can see why Penn's poses a daunting challenge to the flyrodder.

Sparse Grey Hackle alluded to the problem in his *Sports Illustrated* article. Like fine print in a contract, the overlooked warning, "Everyone who knows Penn's Creek agrees emphatically that it is very difficult to fish because the fish are so well fed", was the only sour note he sounded. Cynical Penn's anglers have said that had Sparse dwelt more on that sentence and less on the good fishing, he would have been more accurate!

Fortunately for the angler, not all of the food forms encountered in Penn's Creek are of angling importance. Even so, the list is considerable, and sometimes makes the stream very complex to fish, especially when considering other angling factors. When choosing a fly, an angler must take into account what bugs are in the air around him as well as what may be happening, unseen, in the water in front of him, not omitting criteria based on stretch of stream, water conditions, and time of year. For instance, a June morning in the "Artificials Only" stretch may give good action on #20 Blue Quill dries in slow water, but that same morning can produce even better with #10 *Isonychia* nymphs fished in the riffles. Any clues gleaned from the trout are helpful, but can also be misleading. At times, and I have experienced this fishing wet and dry, individual trout will exhibit selectivity to different feeds.

Paradoxically, and providentially for flyfishers, Penn's Creek adds a redeeming feature to what would otherwise be a difficult task of pattern selection. It is home to many good-sized food forms, including most larger eastern trout stream insects. Better yet, the trout often work them, if not always in a fashion that is readily apparent. Best of all, one or another of these species will be on the water in some way from late April through early November. This is a big plus for flyrodders, who naturally find it easier to use larger sizes. Of course, there is plenty of activity on small flies to be found, and it is sometimes quite good. But why not use big flies if trout will take them? Each year offers plenty of ways to capitalize on this, especially if one is willing to be flexible.

Late winter and early spring often find Penn's running full

◆

Penn's Creek Benefits from 100 years of state conservation efforts.

and cold. The water is difficult to fish, and unpleasant thoughts of a ducking commend caution. Angling pressure is virtually nil, making solitude, if not trout, a sure catch. Even so, those who risk fishing at this time can stumble into good action. During the record snows of 1994, I spoke to one enterprising soul who took his four wheel drive into the "Artificials Only" section. He reported outstanding nymph fishing, "...and the only tracks in the snow were mine."

Those willing to fish Penn's at this time should remember that most of the stream is closed from March 1 to the Opening Day of the regular trout season, pegged every year as the Saturday closest to April 15. Fishing is currently permitted in special regulations waters during the closed season. Check the Summary of Fishing Regulations and Laws that is issued with Pennsylvania fishing licenses for up-to-date information on what portions of Penn's are open, and when, in any given year. Anglers should also note that access can be all but impossible at this time if snow renders mountain roads impassable.

Many small flies hatch in the early months. Winter stoneflies (#10-24) and dark-colored midges (#18-28) often appear in great numbers, but rising activity is usually limited. Nymphs and streamers are a much better ticket for consistent success, and offer a chance at larger fish. Stonefly Nymphs, Crane Fly Larvae, and Sucker Spawn are good bottom-dredgers, with Sculpins and Woolly Buggers serving as good baitfish/attractor patterns.

Late March and early April finds the bug scene picking up. Blue-winged olives (#18) arrive first. But they, along with crane flies (#16) and blue quills (#18) that start in mid-April, are not dependable dry-fly fishing hatches under stream conditions typical for that time of year. Pheasant Tail nymphs can be the best approach for the mayflies, but larger nymph and streamer patterns continue to be flies of first choice for most Penn's flyfishers.

The unexceptional insect activity characterizing Penns' early season changes abruptly after Opening Day, when the Grannom hatch explodes into late April. One day, air over the water carries only some small mayflies. The next day it is filled with swarms of robust, dark caddis—the hatch is on! For the next fortnight, there will not be a time when at least a few, and often a great many caddisflies cannot be seen in stages of emerging, mating, and egg-laying, sometimes all at once. The first heavy hatch of good-sized flies (#12-16), Grannoms get flyrodders charged up, and with good reason, because the Grannom is a daytime hatch and trout work it.

Penn's Creek throws its own peculiar twist into this hatch. During the actual emergence, insects can be so numerous that air over the water's surface seems to vibrate with life, yet relatively few trout can be seen rising. There are simply enough bugs in the water to satisfy the fish. I recall the mournful look on one angler's face as he lamented, "All these flies and not one rise." Now is the time to fish imitations of pupae and drowned adults. Historic patterns from fly fishing's past— Leadwing Coachman and Alder wets—are resurrected to produce excellent results. I have yet to find other patterns that produce for this hatch as consistently as these old standbys, fished deep or with a Leisenring Lift. Later, trout will rise to the egg-laying adults, and some good dry fly fishing can be had by those who scan the water and mark locations of sporadic risers. Hairwing caddis imitations work best then; sometimes it helps to twitch the artificial to mimic the natural's acrobatics.

Hendrickson mayflies (#12-14) often emerge with the Grannom, but Penn's is not a particularly good stream for this popular insect. On other eastern waters, the Hendrickson is considered the height of the season; on Penn's it usually gets lost in the mass of Grannoms. Best action to Hendricksons on Penn's is usually with nymphs and spinners; good fishing with duns is seldom reported.

So exciting is the Grannom that its disappearance, as sudden as its onset, leaves anglers with an almost acute sense of loss. But Penn's is not through for the season, just beginning. For the next two months, a succession of fine hatches roll out, to the delight—and sometimes frustration—of flyfishers. This is prime bug time, and such is the quantity of insects available that trout of all sizes become attuned to aquatics.

In early May more caddisflies show up. A fine large insect, best matched with a tan Elk Hair Caddis (#14) often prompts selective daytime surface feeding. Arriving concurrently is a smaller (#16) olive-bodied caddis, which gives good sport throughout the month. The olive caddis often supplies two shots of activity per day: morning emergence and evening egg-laying. Wets as well as dries work well during these hatches. Pupal and drowned-adult imitations such as the Cowdung nicely complement dry offerings.

March brown and gray fox mayflies also begin in early May. These are excellent fishing hatches on Penn's, although this is not always evident. Instead of hatching en masse, they trickle off, and flyfishers seldom see many except during spinner falls. Their large size (#8-12) and constant appearance does not go unnoticed by trout, however, and fish apparently selective to other flies take notice of the big insects. Predictably, prospecting tactics usually pay off better than fishing the rise, and nymph, wet, and dun patterns all work well. Spinner fishing is problematic, because the naturals have the exasperating habit of swarming—only to disappear at the critical moment! Frustrated flyrodders call this "The Spinner that Never Hits the Water", but the flies actually come down in pocket water, where most are drowned.

Central Pennsylvania's favorite fishing hatches, the sulfur mayflies, make their seasonal debut during the second week of May. A collection of similar species, the sulfurs are renowned for dependability, a long hatch period, and excellent angling opportunities afforded by all life stages. First to appear is one of the largest sulfurs, the Light Hendrickson (#14). It is followed by the Pale Evening Dun (#16), the Pink Lady (#12-14), and the Little Sulfur (#18-20). Hatching begins in daytime, but

March Brown patterns earn their keep at Penn's.

10 p.m. in late May: Bugs still hatching, fish still rising.

grows progressively later as the weather warms, until a point is reached when evening spinner falls occur before the principal dun emergences after dark. A secondary hatch of sulfurs takes place in the morning, and cool, overcast days see afternoon activity.

The sulfurs are a flyfisher's delight, but they are also a challenge. Trout often change from one species or stage of the hatch to another, and even experienced anglers can get caught in the switch. As a result, sulfur patterns have proliferated. "We stock more different patterns and sizes for sulfurs than for any two other hatches put together. This is a clear reflection of their importance on Penn's and the other Central Pennsylvania waters that we service. In fact, our original sign (at Flyfisher's Paradise fly shop) featured a sulfur mayfly." (Steve Sywensky) It pays to carry a wide variety of sulfurs; I have taken trout on imitations of their nymphs, wets, duns, and spinners—all in one day!

By the end of May, evening air traffic over Penn's resembles O'Hare airport. A dozen different mayfly species, plus caddisflies, crane flies, stoneflies, etc., are leaving or returning to the water. Light cahill and *Isonychia* hatches are getting under way, as are a couple of more caddis that have joined the swarm of earlier Trichoptera. But just when fascination with these flies should be at a fever pitch, flyrodders lose all interest in them. For now, at the height of spring, when it does not seem possible or even desirable to add one more insect, Penn's Creek throws the bomb.

The Green Drake Hatch on Penn's Creek

A single event can make a stream's reputation, and if Penn's is known for anything, it is its Green Drake hatch. Over the years the "Shadfly", as the Green Drake is known locally, has become absolutely nailed to Penn's in lore and legend, until the two are almost synonymous. One of our largest mayflies, reaching up to 30-mm in body length, the Green Drake conjures up visions of large trout rising with abandon. It is impossible to understate the effect of this insect, and its connection with Penn's, on anglers' minds. Vacations are planned around it, tackle and flies bought for it, information on it pored over, and the most ridiculous rumors or outrageous lies about it are listened to with gravity. Green drake maniacs just cannot get enough, and start lining up schedules to fish the hatch as soon as they can. In fact, Flyfisher's Paradise begins receiving Penn's/Green Drake queries for next year's hatch while this year's is still going on! The drake's appearance on Penn's sets off a mad rush of flyfishers from a dozen states and foreign countries. Flyrodders crowd the stream, until it is hard to get 50 yards of water to oneself, let alone 10 in the more popular pools. So great is the pull of the Green Drake that nearby waters experience a significant drop in pressure when the hatch is on Penn's. Parking spaces become as hard to find as sites at nearby campgrounds. A carnival atmosphere pervades the stream, in honor of the Shadfly.

A late May afternoon found me sitting on a bridge abutment at Weikert, eating a picnic supper. It was too early for evening action, and I passed the time watching some small bass. A car with New Hampshire plates zoomed onto the bridge and stopped, the driver wildly rubbernecking around. After a moment, the car hurried off. "He'll come back as quick as he went", I deduced, "He's frantic, trying to find the drakes, and that road doesn't follow Penn's." Sure enough, a couple of minutes later the same car ground gravel back. Shortly after, a brownie took up a feeding position below me. I was surprised, it was only 5:30; but I had learned to never ignore nature's signals. If one trout was on the feed, others were too, and I'd better get cracking. The drake fishing started early that evening, and I had a great time.

But many hopeful Green Drake anglers return home disappointed, because Green Drake fishing is not what rumor makes it! It is not a guarantee of good, or even fair action. In fact, the Shadfly presents the toughest challenge of any hatch on Penn's in terms of consistent results. Good fishing can be had with Green Drakes, but it is important to separate fact from fantasy.

The insect's distribution is wide, but relatively few streams in its range have populations, fewer still fishable hatches. The hatch on Penn's was the greatest of them all. "When I came back up here in 1942, I hadn't fished the Green Drake very much. I fished in some northern tier streams back in the late twenties, and had pretty good Green Drake fishing. But when I came down here to Penn's Creek and saw <u>that</u>, I'd never seen anything like it. On most streams the bugs would be up in the trees, you never saw them (after they hatched) close to the ground. But at Penn's Creek they were all right down along the stream, on the bushes and shrubs, packed together like peanuts in a jar." (George Harvey)

Such a hatch did not go unnoticed. "If you wanted to get a spot to fish the Green Drake, you had to go down there and get a spot and sit and wait it out. I used to go down early, down at this side of the tunnel, and sit on a rock to keep other fishermen away from that spot." (George Harvey)

Unfortunately, times have changed. The Green Drake hatch has diminished, a result of siltation from farm and road runoff. But Penn's is still as good a place as any to see the drakes, even though the blizzard hatches of yesteryear are gone, perhaps forever. But while the hatch of insects has declined, the hatch of people has increased, and is now at the point of overload. Sixty-two anglers were counted in one pool during the hatch five years ago, and pressure has not decreased since then. Streamside confrontations, previously unheard of, are starting to happen, and for what?

The Green Drake hatch on Penn's is not a dependable dry fly hatch. Trout often do not rise during the hatch, and then not always to the drakes. When fish do work the Shadfly, it is

◆

The cause of all the commotion: Green Drakes.
Clockwise from top: Green Drake dun; Male spinner; Female spinner.

Green Drake maniacs–This crowd will triple at dusk.

Prime Time hatchboard at Flyfisher's Paradise.

these flights, as the big, white-bodied flies blunder into anglers and the buzzing of thousands of wings is heard. Fishing during the spinner falls is usually less spectacular. Trout often rise very well, but there are just too many flies. There is no doubt that the chief enjoyment derived by flyrodders during coffin fly flights is the show put on by the insects.

George "The Gypsy" Lukas and I hiked halfway to Ingleby that cool, overcast evening. We'd had good fishing to duns earlier in the hatch, and were now out to catch the coffin flies, which we expected to swarm that night. The stream was packed with other flyrodders out chasing the big insects, so we staked out a claim to some water and sat. Because of weather conditions, we didn't have long to wait. At 7:30 the flies started, and kept going like the Energizer Bunny. They flew by in the thousands, then millions, and then millions more! I realized that I was witnessing a great natural spectacle, and just watched. For over an hour the spinners swept by, each intent on the purpose of its upstream flight. Finally, just as darkness settled in, they fell. Trout fed on the rafts of dying insects, and amazingly enough, we caught a few in spite of the naturals' competition. We stayed in the water until almost midnight, and laughed at ourselves on the way out of the woods: "adults" who enjoyed stumbling around a creek at night because fish ate bugs!

As you would expect, much imagination and effort is put into developing productive Green Drake patterns. I have seen some of the most outlandish creations—that worked! Actually, all Green Drake patterns that I have seen have two things in common: they all work; and none of them work all of the time.

Coffin flies.

often after dark or when there are so many naturals that fishing is almost futile. (A word of caution: Do not night-fish on Penn's unless you know the water and are not afraid of snakes and bats!) The stream is crowded during the hatch, and black flies emerge along with the drakes. On the plus side are those occasions when trout actually rise well. At such times it is possible to take big trout that otherwise would not waste their time with insects. The Green Drake is also a good nymph fishing hatch, and my best action with the big bugs is usually subsurface.

Green drakes usually begin emerging in late May, with Memorial Day weekend considered traditional Shadfly time. But dates can change with weather and stream conditions. The hatch makes its first appearance in Union County, and progresses upstream to Coburn. The movement takes a few days, although it can change quickly if weather dictates (it is much more likely to speed up than slow down). Any one point along Penn's will experience 5-7 days of good drake activity, including spinner falls.

Heavy Green Drake mating flights are incredible spectacles. The spinners, nicknamed "coffin flies" after their funereal black-and-white coloration, swarm so thickly that each swing of a fly rod knocks some down. Twilight on Penn's is eerie during

Orange cahill spinner–as pretty as they come.

◆

The large size and active behavior of the natural defies attempts at imitation. The larger the fraud, the more easily it is detected, and even assuming an imitation of perfect size and color, it is not alive and twitching like the real thing.

Like the Grannom caddis, the Shadfly hatch blows out like a candle, leaving only a few stragglers as a final reminder. It seems impossible that so many living creatures should disappear, leaving no indication of their existence, but that is one of nature's mysteries. This is a break point in Penn's year, in stream activity as well as anglers' minds. Many flyrodders feel a letdown after the hatch, and hang up their gear for a while. That is not surprising: the Green Drake is a hard act to follow.

The fall of the last coffin fly ushers in summer fishing on Penn's. The first few weeks see a variety of excellent hatches, some of which continue into fall. Insect activity in the summer is chiefly a function of the weather. The hotter it is, the fewer bugs seen. Likewise, the trout react poorly to heat, and fishing slows as the stream warms. In compensation, pressure dwindles, although it never disappears entirely. Rain and overcast can make for tremendous fishing, sometimes better than the spring afforded. And low, clear summer flows are good conditions for dry fly fishing. Perhaps the most important major change for flyfishers is that evening fishing is compressed into the last half hour, while morning fishing assumes greater significance.

Several flies that started to emerge just before the Green

Drake, but were lost in its magnitude, regain their status. Most visible are light cahills, whose name lumps together a number of different species. Emerging in different shades of yellow and orange, and varying in size from 10 through 16, the cahills provide activity well into fall, although numbers wane as summer wears. Evening fishing is usually the best with Cahill dries, and their spinners (#12-16) should not be neglected, however sparse in number. Cahill nymphs also work well, as Bob Hohn will attest. Bob was fishing a riffle near Ingleby with a cahill

◆

Isonychia mayfly emerging–good sign!

Stonefly shuck–a common summer sight on Penn's.

◆

nymph one June evening, when he took a spill. "When I got up, I picked up my rod, and there was a trout on! That nymph has been a favorite of mine ever since."

Isonychia mayflies are a superb summer hatch in Northcentral Pennsylvania, and they find Penn's much to their liking. These dun-colored mayflies are good-sized (#10-14), have a long emergence span, and offer good fishing in nymph, dun, and spinner stages. Like March Browns, they trickle off the water, and trout are always on the lookout for them. The *Isonychia* is an excellent hatch for prospecting tactics, and during their emergence period flyfishers should not allow apparent lack of numbers to dismay them. In fact, if I were limited to one fly to carry on Penn's in the summer, it would be an *Isonychia* nymph.

Anyone who has picked up rocks in Penn's is aware of its stonefly population. The larger stones begin emergence with the Green Drakes and continue well into the summer. Dry fly fishing is not consistent with stoneflies, but nymph fishing is. As the water gets lower and clearer, stonefly nymphs become less productive, but they are still deadly after a rain.

Large blue-winged olives (#14-16) often go unnoticed on Penn's, but their presence in June and early July brings significant activity. Duns emerge in the morning, especially on cloudy days. Spinners concentrate over fast water in the evening, and can prompt selective feeding.

Caddisflies continue to hatch well all summer long, often eclipsing mayfly action. There are quite a few species, but most can be easily matched with #14-18 olive or tan bodied hair wing dries. Fishing to the rise as well as to the water will bring results. Pupae and drowned-adult imitations also produce, especially in the riffles.

Tricos are not a good fishing hatch on Penns' best water; their bailiwick is upper zone, where trout populations are not as dense. In compensation, blue quill's (#20) appear every day, rain or shine, from mid-June through November. Excepting extremes of hot weather, there is frequently dry fly action for those who follow this emergence. The blue quills small size calls for classic fishing-the-rise tactics, with a premium placed on achieving a drag-free float. Duns and rusty-brown female spinner patterns are the best flies for this hatch.

On the other end of the size scale, yellow drakes (#6-10) provide interesting at- and after-dark fishing. Never present in quantity, yellow drakes can yield results out of proportion to their numbers to flyrodders with good night vision.

Insect activity and fishing slows in the dead of summer, but autumn brings a resurgence of flies and fishing as water temperatures cool. *Isonychias*, cahills, caddis, and blue quills continue to be mainstays of the aquatic insect offering, but a couple of other hatches add icing to the fall bug cake.

The largest caddisfly (#8-10) of Penn's year emerges in the fall. Unfortunately, most hatching takes place at night, but some can be seen on the water in the daytime. This large, orangeish-tan fly gets best results for flyrodders who fish the water with big dries.

A more dependable autumn hatch is one of the smallest of Penns' mayflies, the late olive (#20-26). Beginning in mid-September, olives emerge consistently throughout the fall, and I have seen them as late as December. Fishing their hatches is small fly tactics all the way. By this time of the year every trout in Penn's has seen hundreds of anglers, and survivors are extremely fussy when rising to little flies. The slightest hint of drag, and the game is up. But trout sometimes work olives well, and at such times the effort is worth it.

Fall remains a good time to fish larger flies. Should rain roil the water, streamers can be employed to good effect; they are also useful early in the morning. Big nymphs take trout under the same conditions, with *Isonychia* and stonefly patterns rating as flies of choice.

Penn's ends its insect year where it began, with a few tiny black stoneflies and midges. Flyfishers making their last trip to the stream at this time cannot help but think of the magnificent hatches of the past year, and anticipate next year's.

Tributaries

Penn's Creek has many tributaries, some of which are first-class trout streams in their own right. These streams are well worth investigating when the main stem is not producing. The most popular are the lower portions of Elk, Pine, and Sinking Creeks, which are limestone and/or limestone influenced and offer fair to excellent sport. There are also a great many mountain streams, the best known of which are Cherry Run, Laurel Run, Poe Creek, Swift Run, and Weikert Run, as well as the upper reaches of Elk, Pine, and Sinking Creeks. These are good streams, but will be very frustrating to all but

Green Drake

Coffin Fly

March Brown

Sulphur

Orange Cahill

Blue Dun

Blue Quill Spinner

Dan's Hairwing *Rhyacophila*

Dan's Hair Delta Wing Grannom

Cahill Nymph

Dan's Green Drake Nymph

***Isonychia* Nymph**

Muskrat Nymph

Sucker Spawn

Pale Evening Dun Wet

Dan's March Brown Wet

Leadwing Coachman Wet

Montana Stone

Ted's Stone

Shenk Sculpin

Shenk White Minnow

accomplished fly casters because of their small size and brushy surroundings. Penn's has other, smaller feeders, and most of the tributaries have feeders. I have missed few of these trickles during an obviously well spent fishing career, enjoying every minute on the little gems. But unless you enjoy digging your fly out of hemlocks while swatting mosquitoes and looking out for rattlesnakes, leave the mountain rills alone.

Gear for Penn's Creek

Tackle for Penn's Creek is straightforward. Because of the size of the stream, flyfishers will find long rods much more useful than shorter ones. Five and six weight lines easily handle the diversity of flies and rigs commonly used, with six weight being my preference. Chest waders are a blessing and curse: The water's depth argues for their use, but the demands of walking along Penn's makes their weight and heat fatiguing. Felt soles are a must, and many flyrodders use cleats and/or carry a wading staff. I do not speak lightly, having fallen into Penn's more than any other stream. So have friends, and a former swimming instructor told me about his worst experience, which ended with the words, "I would have drowned had I not let go of my rod." Be careful!

Recommended gear for Penn's does not include float tubes

◆

You can't beat Central Pennsylvania for fall color.

or boats. The water can be run when high, but fishing is usually poor at such levels. During lower flows, boaters will have difficulty negotiating riffles, and draw much verbal abuse from the gauntlet of irritated fishermen they pass through.

Tactics for Penn's Creek

Mark Antolosky and I were unrigging at the end of a day on Penn's. We had caught some fish, thanks to Mark's insights, but hadn't set the world on fire. Another angler approached us in the parking lot. "How'd you guys do?" he queried, and we responded. A tone of frustration marked his next question, "How do you catch fish here?" It transpired that in three trips to Penn's he had yet to see a trout rise, and was beginning to doubt if any were in the stream.

The doleful angler's lament has been echoed by many others over the years. Penn's Creek's varied water types and complex food chain place extra demands on flyrodders. The stream can be extremely disappointing to a "one method" angler who refuses to meet Penn's on its own terms. Flexible flyfishers, however, will enjoy consistent success if they regard fishing as a series of opportunities to enjoy, rather than endure. Every proficient Penn's Creek angler I know has a ready command of several tactics, a working knowledge of the food chain, and is willing to change methods and flies as the stream dictates.

My own experience on the stream bears this up. On those occasions when I stick to a rigid game plan, rewards are usually scant. On the other hand, when I concentrate on what the stream tells me to do—and then do it, I am usually into fish. My days on this waterway seldom see me finish with the same rig that I started with. There is no particular trick or magic fly peculiar to Penn's; tactics and flies that work well on other waters produce here. Just use common sense.

The most dependable method of fly fishing on Penn's is nymphing. Like other limestone streams, its bountiful subsurface life does not encourage the same rising activity found in a similar sized freestone creek. As a result, nymph fishing opportunities are frequent, and Penn's Creek veterans are quick to take advantage of them.

Natural-drift-on-the-bottom is the most productive nymphing method used on Penn's. Flies are cast upstream and allowed to sink and drift with the current, with best results achieved by working straight down one current tongue at a time. This tactic is best employed in the faster water of riffles and heads of pools, high-percentage feeding areas on any stream. It is usually necessary to add weight to the leader to get flies to the bottom quickly and keep them there, and gauging the correct amount of weight is often critical to success. It is also helpful to adjust leader length: The deeper and faster the water, the longer the leader. When in doubt start with a 9-footer and change from there. Tippet size is best determined by water clarity and size of pattern, but 4X seems to offer the best in all-around performance. Strike indicators should not be used as a crutch, but are useful or necessary in certain lies and water conditions. As always, it pays to experiment.

Wet fly fishing is a dying art, but still widely practiced on

Headwaters jewel.

◆

Penn's. When the stream was heavily stocked, wet flies fished down-and-across worked well. Hatchery trout are less drag conscious than wild trout, and full creels often rewarded those who swung wets because it is easy to cover a lot of water with this method. Down-and-across fools fewer fish these days, but wet flies drifted naturally with the current work very well, and can be deadly when fished on the bottom with weight or in tandem with a nymph on the same rig. Wets will also nail rising trout when an appropriate pattern is drifted through their window. Swung wets still have their place, but emphasis should be placed on swinging the flies from the bottom up through a single current rather than shallow and across several currents. Late April through June are the best times to fish wet flies on Penn's. At no other time of the year are so many bugs drifting in the current, and a string of wet flies will often bring good action.

Dry fly fishing is the preference of most flyfishers on Penn's, even though other methods are often more productive. I have paid much attention to the use of sunk flies, but would be the last to discount the effectiveness of dries on this stream. When trout rise, dries can be the most efficient way to catch them.

Fishing the rise is usually the best way to fish dries on Penn's. The time-honored game is played the same here as anywhere else: Find a rising trout, determine what it will rise to, and get a drag free presentation. Failure to achieve the last

point will nullify whatever success you may have in attaining the first two. The best anti-drag aids a dry fly fisherman can have on Penn's, and elsewhere, are a properly constructed leader and the ability to cast in a way that complements it. I highly recommend using George Harvey leaders. When cast correctly, they fall on the water in a series of S-curves that act as a shock absorber to the play of currents, thus inhibiting drag. When choosing a pattern, it pays to be a good observer; I spend more time looking at bugs on Penn's than any other stream. With a good leader and the right fly, all that remains is to have fun locating and fishing to individual risers.

Fishing the water with dries is also fruitful on Penn's, sometimes more so than fishing the rise. Imitations of larger aquatics such as March Browns or *Isonychia*s work well when these flies have been on the water long enough for trout to become accustomed to their presence. Ability in reading the water is of prime importance when prospecting with dries, otherwise much time will be wasted on unproductive spots. It is no surprise that anglers with a long track record on Penn's do best at fishing the water there; past experience guides their casts. Well dressed patterns are best for this type of fishing, where emphasis is placed on keeping the fly on the water; three-hackled adaptations of traditional patterns float better than most. Terrestrials also bring fish up, but are less useful in the big water downstream from Coburn than in the smaller water above town. As with fishing the rise, a drag free float will

41

be your best ally when fishing the water.

Streamer fishing often gets lost in the popularity of nymphing and fishing the hatch, but Penn's is a good place to employ streamer tactics. There are many baitfish present, and larger trout often pound them. Murky water conditions offer the best chance for success with big patterns, and at such times a well-worked streamer can outperform nymphs. As on other waters, fishing the banks and any mid-stream cover will bring the best results. I use two different streamer tactics on Penn's: Cast-and-jerk with streamer and shot strung at intervals along the tippet; and "sculpinating" with Shenk's Sculpins and shot placed immediately ahead of the fly. It pays to cover a lot of water when fishing streamers; trout usually grab the fly on the first cast or two.

Fishing on Penns' Creek:
Read the fine print!

Ernie Erdeky was new to the area, and eager to try Penn's. I took him to a favorite stretch, looking forward to showing him the stream, not to mention showing off a little myself. We nymphed some riffles, each fishing one side. But while Ernie took many trout I took few. My ego was considerably deflated. A couple of weeks later we fished the same water with the same tactics, under similar stream conditions. This time I racked up the bigger score.

A good command of tactics does not guarantee success of Penn's Creek, even when coupled with intimate knowledge of the stream and its food chain. Fishing there always means fishing, but not necessarily catching. Instead, luck still seems to play a role. Those who regularly fish the stream comment,

almost lovingly, on the whimsical way Penn's bestows fortune.

Fly Patterns for Penn's Creek

A flyfisher could go broke buying every last pattern called for by Penn's cornucopia of food forms, and a fly tier would have a full-time job supplying the demand. Fortunately, and as on other waters, a smaller list of flies will suffice to produce a satisfying season on Penn's. My list is extensive, but includes the very full range of sizes that I have used in the past on the stream. One or two sizes of each fly will adequately equip most Penn's Creek flyfishers.

Nymphs: Montana Stones (4-12), Ted's Stones (6-12), Blue Quill (14-18), Pheasant Tail (12-18), Dark Sulfur (12-14), Light Sulfur (14-16), Light Cahill (10-14), Green Drake (8), Walt's Worm (8-14), Muskrat Nymphs (12-16), Casual Dress (2-10), Sucker Spawn (12-16), Green Weenies (12-14).
Many of these nymphs can be tied as bead-heads.

Wet Flies: Leadwing Coachman (10-16); Dan's Brown Wet (8-16); Pale Evening Dun (12-16); Light Cahill (8-14); Orange Cahill (10-14).

Mayfly Duns: Blue Quill (14-20), Red Quill (14-18), Blue-Winged Olive (14-24), Hendrickson (12-14), March Brown (10-12), Gray Fox (10-12), Sulfur (12-18), Light Cahill (10-14), Orange Cahill (10-16), Green Drake (6-10), *Isonychia* (10-14). Traditional and Sparkle-Dun patterns are both useful.

Mayfly Spinners: Spinner patterns that correspond to the

◆

Montana Nymphs work in Pennsylvania, too.

If only we put this much thought into our work!

◆

aforementioned duns are a necessity throughout the season.

Caddisfly Adults: Grannom Caddis (12-16), Tan Caddis (8, 14-18), Olive Caddis (14-18). I like using my own Hair Delta Wing style of tie.

Midges: Griffith's Gnats (20-24), Cream Midges (24-28).

Terrestrials: Hair Ants (10), Crowe Beetles (12-16), Letort Crickets (14-16), Wet Ants (8-16), Wet Inchworms (12-14).

Streamers: Black Woolly Buggers (4-8), Black Shenk's Sculpins (4-10), Shenk's White Minnow (4-8).

There are many other patterns well worth trying. Every fly-rodder on Penn's has favorites, many of which are the result of years of experience and experimentation.

Accommodations, Fly Shops, Guide Services, and Points of Interest

Flyfishers traveling to Penn's Creek should remember that the watershed is largely rural. There are few streamside services to satisfy immediate needs, and it is necessary to make arrangements for tackle, licenses, lunch, gas, and water before going fishing. Accommodations, ranging from rustic campgrounds to elegant Bed-and-breakfasts, are easier to find and accustomed to angling clientele.

Bed-and-Breakfast

The Brick House, One Hundred East Aaron Square, Aaronsburg, PA 16820 (814)349-8795

Centre Mills, HCR Box 210, Rebersburg, PA 16872 (814)349-8000
Guests staying at Centre Mills have the privilege of fishing a private stretch of Elk Creek, which flows through the property. Hostess Maria Davidson has made this establishment one of Pennsylvania's top angling B&Bs. This is a sentimental favorite of mine; my wife, Lynn, and I spent our wedding night here.

General Potter Farm, R.D. 1 Box 135, Spring Mills, PA 16875 (814)238-1484
This B&B is located on Route 322 in Potters Mills.

Jane Green House, 209 West Aaron Square, Aaronsburg, PA 16820 (814)349-8118
Breakfast not included, but guests permitted use of kitchen for breakfast, lunch, and dinner.

Woodward Inn, P.O. Box 177, Woodward, PA 16882
Also houses The Hummingbird Room, a four-star restaurant (reservations only)
The Woodward Inn is the closest B&B to the "Artificials Only" section of Penn's Creek and the upper reaches of Pine Creek. It is located on Route 45 in Woodward. One of the innkeepers, John Doren, is a fly fisherman, and can be of much assistance with directions. His wife, Chris, is an excellent cook.

◆

A delight to your eye: Wild brown and sparkling water.

43

Penn's flat water is beautiful and challenging.

Campgrounds

Hemlock Acres Campground, P.O. Box 31, Coburn, PA 16832 (814)349-5955
Rustic and improved sites, cabins. This campground is located off the old Millheim Pike, which crosses Penn's Creek upstream from Coburn.

Penn's Creek Campground, R.D. #1, Box 195H, Millmont, PA 17845 (717)922-1371
Improved sites, rental trailer available. This campground is located off the Penn's Creek Road downstream from Weikert.

Poe Paddy State Park, c/o Reeds Gap State Park, R.R. 1, Box 276-A, Milroy, PA 17063-9735 (814)349-8778
Rustic sites.

Poe Valley State Park, c/o Reeds Gap State Park, R.R.1, Box 276-A, Milroy, PA 17063-9735 (814)349-8778
Rustic sites.

Union County Sportsmen's Club, R.D. 1, Box 406, Millmont, PA 17845 (717)922-1128
Improved sites, restaurant open to public Wed-Sun. The club is located on the Penn's Creek Road outside of Weikert. Ring the doorbell for admittance.

◆

Grannom caddis and imitation.

Cottages and Trailers

The Country Centre, R.R. 1, Coburn, PA 16832 (814) 349-4359
Trailers, sandwiches, general store, fishing licenses, guide service.

Musick's Modern Cottages, P.O. Box 50, Aaronsburg, PA 16820 (814)349-8316
Cottages.

Fly Shops and Guide Services

Angling Fantasies, Box 1294, R.R. 2, Port Royal, PA 17082 (717)527-2805 or (717)543-5481
Insured guide service. The oldest, most experienced guide service in the area, Angling Fantasies offers trips to many Central Pennsylvania waters. Partners Jim Gilson and Dave McMullen have been fishing Penn's Creek for decades, and are well versed on the idiosyncrasies of the stream. Both men have received numerous mentions in angling publications.

The Feathered Hook, Main Street, Coburn, PA 16832 (814)349-8757
Thomas & Thomas, Redington, flies, tackle, guide service, fly tying and fishing schools, bed-and-breakfast. Founded in 1989, The Feathered Hook is owned by Jane and Jon Witwer, an Ohio couple who liked the area enough to settle here. Jon guides and instructs fly tying and fishing.

Flyfisher's Paradise, 2603 East College Avenue, State College, PA 16801 (814)234-4189 FAX (814)238-3686
Orvis, Cortland, Sage, Loomis, Metz Distributor, limited guide service, group and individual schools in fly fishing, specialty fly fishing, and fly tying. Phone, FAX, and mail order. One of the East's premier fly shops, Flyfisher's Paradise stocks more quality fly fishing and fly tying supplies than all other businesses in Centre and surrounding counties put together, as well as offering a full range of instructional services. Founded in 1974, it is owned and operated by Steve Sywensky (recipient of First Annual George Harvey Master's Award for Excellence in teaching fly tying) and Dan Shields (author, guide, FFF—certified Fly Casting Instructor, fly tying instructor). Staff includes Walt Young (photographer, guide, First Place Champion Pennsylvania and New Jersey State Fly Tying Competitions, 1995 Pennsylvania Fly Tier of the Year), Doug Wennick (guide), and Mark Antolosky (Guide, former Wulff School instructor). Flyfisher's Paradise is conveniently placed to service all streams in Pennsylvania's northern limestone region.

Hotel and Motel

Autoport Motel, Business Route 322, State College, PA 16801 (814)237-7666
Rooms, restaurant, coffee shop, bar.

Millheim Hotel, Main Street, Millheim, PA 16854 (814)349-5994
Rooms, restaurant, bar.

Points of Interest

Penn's and Woodward Caves offer an unusual break from fishing, as well as a glimpse into the forces that created the Penn's Creek fishery. The Mount Nittany Inn commands a fine view of Penn's Valley.

Penn's Cave, R.D. 2, Box 165A, Centre Hall, PA 16828 (814) 364-1664
Cave tours, airfield, airplane tours, snack bar, wildlife preserve. Penn's Cave is a water cavern, and offers a singular experience.

Woodward Cave, Route 45, Woodward, PA 16882 (814)349-9800

Cave tours, campground, snack stand.
Closest Point on Penn's Creek: Coburn.
Woodward Cave is located off Pine Creek Road, which intersects Route 45 in Woodward. On occasion, choral groups perform in the cave; such events are well worth attending.

Mount Nittany Inn, R.D. 2, Box 322, Centre Hall, PA 16828 (814)364-9363
Bed-and-breakfast, dining.

Bugs aren't the only hatch at Penn's in late spring.

The Future of Penn's Creek

Penn's Creek is at a critical crossroads. Up to now, the stream's natural resources have enabled it to maintain a viable fishery in the face of man's depredations. But demands on the watershed continue to escalate, and may ultimately prove too much for the fishery to sustain its present quality.

Farming and development pushing out from State College will continue as the watershed's largest sources of non-point pollution and water removal. Road construction and maintenance also hurt, through carelessness in State and local planning and execution of projects, herbicide spraying of shoulders, and winter salting. The biggest threat of all looms as proposed quarrying operations threaten siltation and disruption of the water table.

Not all is doom and gloom. Some farmers are fencing cattle out of streams, and many are learning to use nutrients and soil management wisely, rather than haphazardly. Sewage treatment in the watershed is improving, with Millheim and Spring Mills, scheduled to begin treatment soon. Most important, residents are showing greater awareness of Penn's Creek's eco-

nomic and aesthetic values, and a coincident willingness to defend them. They will have to work hard to preserve the stream: The future is upon them.

Penn's Creek can be changed for the better, and a good first step is to prevent further degradation. A program of land and easement acquisition on the watershed is in its infancy; any land so protected will bear much fruit for the whole drainage. A moratorium on dam building on main stem and tributaries is also needed to maintain flows. Future road building and maintenance must take ground and surface water into account.

Active steps for restoration are likewise needed. Reforestation, where possible, should be encouraged, especially with conifers. Farmers can be encouraged, without coercion, to implement beneficial changes in pasturing and runoff management. Parts of the stream are in urgent need of bank stabilization; it will be necessary to carry out large-scale stream improvement projects to accomplish this. Some dams and farm ponds can be breached without economic loss to the landowners; accomplishments in this vein will greatly help Penns' fishery. These steps will take time and effort, but must happen if future generations are to enjoy what we have.

Anglers who love their sport must work to maintain the resource. Those interested in preserving Penn's can do so by joining the Penn's Valley Conservation Association, which focuses on watershed protection. This group is one of the hardest-working conservation groups I have seen, and has been instrumental in leading the fight against proposed quarrying operations. Memberships and donations (including tax-deductible donations for land purchases and easements) can be sent to:

Penn's Valley Conservation Association
P.O. Box 165
Aaronsburg, PA 16820

Bane of dogs and camps.

In Conclusion

Fishermen looking for "easy pickings" will not find them at Penn's Creek. Instead, they will encounter on of the toughest angling classrooms in existence. Even the most skilled fly-rodder has no guarantee of success on this stream. On the other hand, those who enjoy a challenge, and are willing to work at angling and observation skills will find Penn's rewarding.

Too many years ago, I spent an Indian summer getting to know Penn's. The stream had been familiar in places, but unknown as a whole to me. I began my exploration at the lower boundary of trout water, and worked my way up. Each day found me starting where the previous day's fishing had ended.

What began as a busman's holiday for a partner in a fly shop turned into a love affair that glorious autumn. As I fished each stretch, unaccompanied by any save birds and deer, I became enamored of the stream and its surroundings. Each little spring seep, each run and rock, each wild brownie caught or hinted at, offered another insight into what makes this won-

Penn's has plenty of pocket water.

◆

derful troutway tick. Each peep through one of these windows revealed more than just another facet of nature: there was present a sense of the jewel in entire. By the end of my sojourn, Penn's Creek had captivated me with its abundant charm.

◆

Penn's Creek: A jewel in the beautiful Pennsylvania woods.